# this hall of several tortures
reuben woolley

Newton-le-Willows

Published in the United Kingdom in 2020
by The Knives Forks And Spoons Press,
51 Pipit Avenue,
Newton-le-Willows,
Merseyside,
WA12 9RG.

ISBN 978-1-912211-53-1

Copyright © Reuben Woolley, 2020.

The right of Reuben Woolley to be identified as the author of this work has been asserted by them in accordance with the Copyrights, Designs and Patents Act of 1988. All rights reserved. No part of this publication may be reproduced, stored in a retrieval system, transmitted in any form or by any means, electronic, photocopying, recording or otherwise, without prior permission of the publisher.

**Acknowledgements:**

Some of these poems first appeared in the following magazines: *The Interpreter's House, Lighthouse, Laldy Journal, Proletarian Poetry, The Otolith, Ink Sweat & Tears, The BeZine* and *The Writer's Cafe.*

I should also like to thank Pamela Ireland and Jessica Mookherjee for their valuable comments on an earlier version of the manuscript.

*for Fran Lock, Jerry Rothenberg and Antony Owen*

# contents

| | |
|---|---|
| this hall of several tortures | 9 |
| turn the page over she said | 13 |
| another blue requiem | 14 |
| tell me a life tell me a story | 15 |
| lost words | 17 |
| hollow bones she saw | 19 |
| playing new games | 21 |
| continuous performances | 22 |
| lately a time she said | 24 |
| these sundry openings | 25 |
| unknown divas & other consequences | 26 |
| white noises | 28 |
| anonymous displeasure | 29 |
| listening to lions | 31 |
| unloving | 32 |
| undistressed she sings | 34 |
| deadground | 36 |
| holes within holes she digs | 37 |
| imagine an architecture / imagine a wall | 38 |
| the logic of not moving | 39 |

| | |
|---|---|
| blue addiction | 40 |
| come quiet now | 41 |
| home flight or none | 42 |
| soft organs & hardcore | 44 |
| breaking atlantis | 45 |
| time comes counting / one two zero | 46 |
| dry flesh growing | 47 |
| ground ivy & breathing oh dionysus | 48 |
| virginia's move | 49 |
| the places between | 50 |
| reason is a foreign beast | 51 |
| a passing or not the smoke screens | 53 |
| preterite anatomy | 55 |
| the weighing of silences | 57 |
| shining through screens | 58 |
| palaeontology.look | 60 |
| elsewhere I breathe | 61 |
| so poor a process | 62 |
| two ways out | 63 |
| distance between | 64 |
| the tide she leaves in disarray | 65 |
| transformations / she didn't see | 66 |
| deeper rivers | 68 |
| nothing is she said | 69 |

| | |
|---|---|
| downstream & almost dry | 70 |
| a failing orbit she chooses | 71 |
| she said she said | 73 |
| & neither a refuge | 74 |
| cutting through thin parallels she does | 75 |
| bedded & bleeding | 76 |
| a tawse / a cleansing | 77 |
| sharp myths she plays | 78 |
| floating in cold water | 80 |
| are imperceptual she saw | 81 |
| alarums don't bring rain she knows | 82 |
| turn a hole what else does she do | 83 |
| came lightning she saw | 85 |
| time to go never she cries | 86 |
| double histories | 88 |
| ultimate simulations | 90 |
| descry a world / a world she cries | 92 |
| sand count | 93 |
| singularities i cannot touch she confesses | 94 |
| words i don't hear she said | 95 |
| sweet dreams she whispered | 96 |
| they walk the way they go she said | 98 |
| party decorations | 99 |
| closing doors on present spaces | 100 |

reuben woolley

# this hall of several tortures
*(with thanks to Fran Lock)*

in all the houses

unhiding

don't you hear
my coldsong

                                                  she cries

not
open
a door
an eveningbell

i'll pay you
in cuts
        your pound
& counterweight

        a blessing
& greyblood dancing
on thirsty ground

                                              & she
                                              names everything
                                              she sees

in amber all &
i'll wear it
round my scrawny neck

## this hall of several tortures

you
tore out
my speaking
        throat
                                  she writes
                deeper
                now

the still
        between

come to the sundering
piece / the
jugular dreams of distance

                here
for me / finding
words not long
enough for any comfort

          & now you can
a wilful dance where
time's away & out
                                she hears a song

            i don't sing
this
pretty step for hollow
graves.the angled faces
share a tale / flailing
my ghost
me
      fool unholy fool unweeping

reuben woolley

              here
be no sense
when land unfreezes

the flowing dark
              shine
in the screaming.they carry
a broken
          lie / a while
they say.they hold
                it
              down
certain to count these needle-points
the thieves of little meanings

are things inside
i haven't excised.my almost
stories left
behind / the fall of atoms.see
it voluntarily

in this time / where
it bears still fully
          fools &
consent the tired lands

this old talk / it
loses us
& words can end
in smoke & ash.oh marry this
on quiet nights when
            fevers
are not normal

## this hall of several tortures

        slow
we're talking
somewhat truth / the loss
of all my lucent voices

                                    she says

they quiver

how high
& weight are unimportant
we do not measure breath

or earthbeat.watch

me walk
in my present skin / a fallen
face                                 she will remove
            see each
my soft disguises

       i don't need
eyes
or fingers not here
in empty rooms where
only we can see
through bone

i won't be
        sliced
off stupid.not
dying

       not hardly

i dance on horizons
& don't cast shadows

reuben woolley

# turn the page over she said

the holes the holes do not come
empty.i dig through a time
a matter coincides

& we occupy the room together.who said
she could not fold a world
away & bring another
skin / another tired foundling

in our dark shells &
never speaking.oh the shit
of it all on both our sides

we scratch a putrid sore
in our reflections
& bleed a waiting speech
on the earths of undelight

this hall of several tortures

# another blue requiem

see this she says
my autonomous shadows dancing

                                        distant

from any sun i know / a different step

                  & still

                      december

are lights
in all these histories &

                children
grow old & die
just the same                                               she says

reuben woolley

# tell me a life tell me a story

colour
is just a life away a
skull's story

                the yellow
dog moon pocked & smiling
like tomorrow i gather
horizons for time

                  let's see
the fit the fumbling / the
dust on my shoes like anyone might
confuse a connection / the language
of my finger pointing the change
of somebody's truth
                      it's a sliding
scale / a trill on an off-beat it leaves
my raw new flesh to hold.i'll
pretend we know me
                      not flaming
again there are better extremes
where i carry whales in my hand

not raining /
        / a mote may glow
in this lost
i do        idle
as catch can.waking
was not wasted

## this hall of several tortures

                      & the old pimp wants
his price / a life is not sufficient

daughter that's no river
how far we cast our eyes
this isn't venice deeper
on other clients' beds

so charon sells tears now the aching bastard
we don't forget a fucking john his mad master
sowing barren                                         she said

# lost words

meaning

        i do

& counting.refusals
are caged for protection

is a weather
inside / a slight
slip in the words i use

                                        & why she sings
                                            she does

a voice a storm i know

a people / a very
forget me now i am not
here & always crazy like
everything's turning come throw
me down when time was solid i haven't
space

        enough

for quietude

## this hall of several tortures

tell me now
a new direction
& fuck the sound of it all.i could never
write in tune i lost the key the poor
clock wind me down in dust & toothless

reuben woolley

# hollow bones she saw

again no
start
nor unfortunate steps.see them eclipse a light
            she said

i'm dancing still
  in here

   frozen

like all machines.it's some
kind of heaven i'm expecting
wings &
featherless
in streets.there's no
room for breathing & talk
is no comfort at all

     bridge

     this

     away

     it
could have stopped before
a knife

## this hall of several tortures

      so find
my stupidity
unmoving
         & wearing
a history mask / these
bones agree

let's capture stray

        atoms

just dust / just floating

      just waste

reuben woolley

# playing new games

like here
it's different

                                            she said

slightly

to one side
a shift / another
name & what
that follows

i hesitate
a second for others
call my name.i don't

            respond / it isn't

me in party frock & all
made up.the fuck
it's happening
it's not my earth

> this hall of several tortures

# continuous performances

when the screen         changes
it comes
    in slow

       motion

another flow
of liquid

     record

come bleed on me
the flicker tape

                                    she said

i haven't chosen
yet this world
just
    turn the dial
    a little
       a way

i haven't found
the line to fill

                                    she said

       still

reuben woolley

i search
in all the vast
      empires
you think you'll name
as things come round again

| this hall of several tortures |

# lately a time she said

                                                                               she speaks a world
                    remember

where
still they're dead & i'm

not
starting        anything
nor unfortunate

              help

there are stones
which hold the earth

            together

            be

tree
     bending

& key this
in e minor    is

leaves

        falling

# these sundry openings

        there is space

                outside

                        she said

where gorgons walk
in comfort

& razor-
wire
is no border.oh
their gaping mouths

        combing snakes.i
        bleed for them

        what else
        can i leave

        was never mine

& space
    there is
        where
            rain dissolves all traces
            & even graves go into hiding

this hall of several tortures

# unknown divas & other consequences

    i wear
           me

              invisible

the many voices
at grief &

              disposal

                      a
geography of monsters

we

don't visit
not ever in tears

                  i stepped
sidewards
into a day
& even in slow
all the
        tawdry
stitched together.he was
dancing in his teeth / is
still

a silence

        shouting

my desperate
crazy so tired & these bodies
a tapestry of strange
i survive in occlusion

this hall of several tortures

# white noises

she wears her shoes
        uncertainly
in every frequency

opens wormholes        maybe
while i is unsure

& words fold
in
on
        this
        her shining dance
        of {possibles}

she holds space
in the time of her hands

where she build worlds
each moment        another story

# anonymous displeasure

here i am
at

    angles
from myself

don't you know
where we

      live
        the same

      separate
the decisions / a chosen
skin / a membrane

        tight

our crazy earths
                                she said
stoking
an unquiet life

we also have bombs
where is no terrain for mutual delight

## this hall of several tortures

                    oh
paint
another garden

black the grass &
black the space between

# listening to lions

these are version

                                      she said

& the old ones know
                murmuring
through their bones

quick moves aren't part
of any story.we tell
the oak song
& the mountains

the rest are mud
slides & flies / hurrying
to a dry drowning

> this hall of several tortures

# unliving

i can't leave
carelessly.the doors
close

                                                                          she said

    & even
the judges are wary

this hunger
of lost times
& my papers
aren't in order

there's nothing
different.here
there is &
here there's none

it is an equaliser

                                                                          she said

on any plane you find / a strange
geometry

       & i
can be

perhaps

      i'm always
trying to reverse
a glass image / a
swollen belly

this hall of several tortures

# undistressed she sings

    let's leave

               cold

    together                                 she said

    it's another song
    of crushed glass
    & swallowing

          an accidental state

              & darkly
    paint a time / a tall
    tree here.it
    cries its pain i wear

    & walk
    in all this ageing splendour.stray

    parts we are
    on an old grey day

    it's a game
    of opening wings

               like
    everything else it's done

at distance

       white marble
       black feathers

> this hall of several tortures

# deadground

comfort
comes in drabs
                                      she said

& flatlined.any move
is accidental

                still

i see
a routine / headstone
or nothing at all

                    chain
feeding on the soft

                    remains
& where they are
                                she didn't say

reuben woolley

# holes within holes she digs

trash
& trinkets i found
in dust / the crumbled
walls

where i cannot fully
see a space / an open
story of possible

hidden

between

ah fuck the sender
such

news

repeats
the tremors

bring

down

the gilt & murals
all.this
                                        she said
i'll continue
with fingers & nails

this hall of several tortures

# imagine an architecture /
# imagine a wall

we spread

      deserts

where we walk

                                                   she saw

it's no
        slight
            coincidence.we
complete a task

say

we determine this sand
in
              straight
              lines & arches

build
a city

& it's almost real

reuben woolley

# the logic of not moving

& where's a world
                    she asked
          concerned
a step or back.there's
no straight road.i'll take
the notes / let them
run but

coda me this.the pulse
of all the hiding / the
silent breaths of fear

they've built walls
here in my head

| this hall of several tortures |
|---|

# blue addiction

oh well

they played those blues

      sweet

            she said

let a long

  note

  sound

it's where they are
right now / & a fearful
side

we'll bury it
in smoke & liquid

they say

inject a sad
smile

# come quiet now

i've acquired                time
a little
                                          she said
& limited

          sight / a

          parallel

of spare limbs

this wilful toy
i take
through smooth
cities.let's
manoeuvre me a

                    space.find
paths in all the growth
of skin / the hard
              divide & let me open
doors where there are none

 i'll pay with cells
                                          she promised

& see a smaller life
where i can lie

`this hall of several tortures`

# home flight or none

there's light
round corners
where

stories

go missing

                                                             she said

            & we
survive accepted
faces.say turbulence
is normal

               tell me
where
a body
hides when time
comes squealing

now
through tremors
these
      shining
            ruins we live
            don't ask
for lies they
surely come.we're

        bleeding

out for real.is no tv film
just leave it all in pieces.the

               red

flowers
blooming
& shrapnel
for hopscotch

this hall of several tortures

# soft organs & hardcore

here
      they come
dead from above
            uncrowned
         & still

                           it is the dark
                           she brings

they steal they say they
split the empty

      space

      they chew
an old life / an earth
too many
for such thin skins

where difference is slight

a null breath
they excise a lung or more.it gives
this much

                           this much
                           she leaves

            sputum

& a red-lip memory

# breaking atlantis

came a wind
                                          she said
i did i heard it

            singing
through dark & a broken piano

i don't know
the words.this world
                              strings
different in its disguise

they talk at me
in counter rhythm.cross

a heart & maybe foul

                        let me
bleed in a drowning street

reuben woolley

> this hall of several tortures

# time comes counting / one two zero
*(for Antony Owen)*

when the rain comes
in shadows

                                            she said

i'll see the worlds
turn
like pages

               the skins
they left
on walls / on
pavements

               my
nagasaki
heroes / my
hiroshima angels

they'll not see
not yet / not ever

& the cherry trees still flower

tears for generations

reuben woolley

# dry flesh growing
*(for the victims in yemen)*

a body

        the long water
i don't sail.said sands
to meet & scattered
bones walking

        here be monsters

                deep

i'll sing it again.this is no
shanty say bells goodbye

& children sink the same
i see.spill
your money in shrapnel
my silent voices.food
is no necessity an empty
belly fills the picture

too late she said

this hall of several tortures

# ground ivy & breathing oh dionysus

there an under

        story / a
tangled state &

            cruel

in dead

   shade

       where
a chorus
dismays / a slip
of single voice

                she said

i can't read
with these eyes / tell me

who survives
the last page

you cut here & open
let the words
bleed out

## virginia's move

who said
the town was burning

                                          she saw

the smoke
from every side of it
& the faces

the screaming mouths.we'll have
a taste of it

              & every difference
is marked for onslaught

it's time
                                      she said

for removal /
      /
            / for a stirring
from the alleys

this hall of several tortures

# the places between

it's this
wavering time

                                                        she said

            i see the fine
membranes
trembling /
        / the thin
reflections of
twisted orders

a free disguise
                when nothing's
on offer

        even

& the swollen bellies
of empty

i don't want to
watch the greasy rivers

where plagues
come in buckets

# reason is a foreign beast

in that country
they turn time

                                            she said

consider the sand i know

                falling

through seconds.it is
a life i declare

they sail
to the edge of their flatness.travel

a day's
work / a
journey

i know

                                            she said

i'm watching
through thin
screens & cutting
screams

| this hall of several tortures |

& they bury their dead
in green land

don't they

# a passing or not the smoke screens

walking on cinders
                                         she is
a fine gown of flame.i'll sing

you a blood song where
light comes
               displaced / heal
in your nightmares.it's no
vain promise

             trace
me the paths
with delicate / untread
these burning veins

               where
all the dead
have different voices
& personal

how i am myself
in ash

        the wind
threatens & trembles no
pleasure here the story
stays
the palette hardens these

## this hall of several tortures

bags of bones
& chemistry & nothing
is new.i'm

         wearing
stars on my feet

             buried
in numbers
a grave moon

          & no one's
waiting in my years i'm rooted
in all my long-lying

           confused
           by distance
                        she's
                        conspicuously
                        absent

          a sky
is very close today i see
silence we are always ending

reuben woolley

# preterite anatomy

there were sharper
cuts

                  a while ago
                                  she murmured

coming not
a distance &
counting

the loops of
every skin

            peeled

a globe
opens

it's
a different day
for wearing

              a new
face.i'm
taking off the shine
again
they come to see

## this hall of several tortures

     the bleedings
      a cup to catch
      the final drops

i'll take me now
i have a crutch
for kindling.i'll not
want for cold

            she said

    this
is terminal

& i
am working on it

# the weighing of silences

watch them
           step
            through
& let a gravity
take them

cold

                                                          she said

this space

      between & i

watch them
where they don't talk
in the thickness of it &

cold

                                                          she whispered

this matter of their
daily words not coming

this hall of several tortures

# shining through screens

                                            if she looks
                                            she

won't

see through
moves / a light
step / a broken
song

                                          she doesn't miss

       the
zero surrounds

               & distance
is an object / a
failing encounter

they waltz on edges
cutting

       deeply
in time they
wander

                                        & does she
                                        remark

the slow
diversion

the fine sanding of surfaces

this hall of several tortures

# palaeontology.look
(for a yazidi girl)

the uneyed face of home

                she cries

a deeper red / they filmed
her sharply
                stones crush
all
order out of flesh
& she counts
truths in fractions / can't
integrate
                this

unwhole
                & dying
i have no doubt

there are no names
in such
                a thousand
granite    flint      sand
what will our fossils say

& she is silent

very loudly

reuben woolley

# elsewhere i breathe

it could have been different
& not this
        slow dust

        over

        empty.let's see
a finger            fumbling
too tired to change
a stuttering mess.look
at my confusion i cannot
bleed sufficient i say
these crazy details don't hear
a lonely word i breathe you
this repeat

        somewhere
i have my own name now
reassembling
another history i don't know
& never hanging words
like plaster geese.remember

            they are still
            dead & quietly

            december

this hall of several tortures

# so poor a process

where this mind
        sinks
i'll be weary

                                              she declared

& how
do they do
this         repeat
how
do they know

a bitter find

i haven't risen
to further
patterns / outline
darker words / the crap

                lying

undisturbed.roll
a hook
in guts / the faecal
matter fathomed

& even tired minds
can close the shutters

# two ways out

this is not my skin
i see
                                                          she said

        hanging
in disorder

& the old
   the bones

are not my own

               a neck
is a delicate thing

stretched &

twisted

      it is
not me.i drown
in sweet illusion singing

oh rivers
keep me young

this hall of several tortures

# distance between

sewing together
every lasting piece
           i make
a rose
      on folds
      on leaves

here's a bloodthorn
& the lines.paint
ages / flowers
    & faces
everything fades.it is
the nature of dark
glass
      reflecting

& we'll dance
a lost tango late
               & lips
tire in substance.just see
the words lie deceiving
      like petals
      like blood
like smiles on old canvas

reuben woolley

# the tide she leaves in disarray

yesterday is stemmed
in my ascendancy

                                                she said

these cuts are precision
for each release
                a water memory

blood not
tears.i'm not
at home

        anywhere

to pass these words
the multiple deaths so
eloquently

                insatiable

let's amble another day
i have forgotten
& faded all these shabby echoes
where i don't believe

a simple thing.your
handshakes in the rain / waves
in asphalt singing
her seas of dust

## this hall of several tortures

# transformations / she didn't see

learning

to fit

in theory

                she thought

they see
a place in all
the foolish moves

& where the faces
show a different
line they

        paint

an old expression

don't wait

        patient

you can slap it on
thick / shining
just like yesterday

                                                   she said

there's no
fucking change

not a fucking chance

this hall of several tortures

# deeper rivers

it's dry earth

    or flood

                    she murmured

there's no
    easy
way & roads
are doubtful

the drowned bones / the skulls

for landfills

an overlap
   of screams / a
final rattle

arrhythmic

reuben woolley

# nothing is she said

i'm not now this sky
this
        dark

space &

where i am
in null
   endeavour

                     she whispered

let me find
a different

door.this

hesitation

a shuffle elsewhere
a marked departure

          oh

so slowly

this hall of several tortures

# downstream & almost dry

    there are spaces
    where people live
        & things

                            she doesn't dream
                            a flight

& this
is not
a weeping cut      a knife
                    mistake

                          she walked the quiet
                          rooms where
                          steps
                          were swallowed      ready
                          for going

don't leave your signposts here

                north

is just a brief description

listen to the river

# a failing orbit she chooses

        & how
the sun travels
           this one.choose

       i cut
strings / set cores to

          dangle

curious

                                              she wonders

        this
i am &
all my other
      varied
beings where

             space

comes

gliding

oh my slighthood
did you ever

            really

## this hall of several tortures

break a glass / see
a cracked body
in lost hours when

speech

    becomes
unstable & such

a scarce landing
to the north of ourselves a
white sky & a shrinking demeanour

# she said she said

look

                        she said

their
normal / the way
they walk their killing
steps.watch
them in ashes

false

golden.i'll see
their

hunger

real

too often.a crazy
dance / a cutting move

                        she said

it's time to go now
& close
the last worming door

this hall of several tortures

# & neither a refuge

walls it is / a
bloodless home

        a house                she owns

          i
looked in the dust &
broken webs
         tell me
where a window is to see
a life they walk
the rutted paths

come crawl
from crater.i'll wrap you
in a sweet / a biting shroud

reuben woolley

# cutting through thin parallels she does

i'm always crossing

        frontiers

                                  she said

whether it be cold or
whatever might happen
when you step on lines

i'm not here
      for
forms to follow.i'll open
other doors

                                she promised

no skins
        between
the hiding

i'll take a knife
& pare away dead matter

this hall of several tortures

# bedded & bleeding

i have far to go

                                            she thinks

in scarcity
i am & this
is not mine

flesh is another

       story

i read with my eyes
my own

                                          she says

there is no reception / no
                / free offering

where i live.it's not
my home

& even my blood
          falls
on demand

## a tawse / a cleansing

behind the walls
they beat out
their
      cruel

steps

                          she stated

& all the sins
of their mothers / their faces
are perfect now unsmiling
              i don't know
the time of birth / the
hour
of death

& silken
shrouds they
will not have

these walls

          still

silence in their religion

this hall of several tortures

# sharp myths she plays

am echo

    impartial

                                                    she said

they sound in me
the idle
       reflections

& i can't play
those games i don't
understand

                watch
them fall
in failing action
their voices
        breaking

        even air

& i
repeat

                                            she said

i repeat
their futile dreams
narcissus you are

skin
beautiful

& oh

    such

        pain

this hall of several tortures

# floating in cold water

breathing thickly
they do
        like swimming
in
air

    & how
the bodies fill.they'll
pull me
to corners
        retiring.i'll
hide with you

    shining

    through / the
wracked breath

don't

    waste

    my words

                      she said

they are not easy / twisted
        / i'll deal with me
feel
the waves come tumbling.can
you taste the flood

# are imperceptual she saw

i see

                                                she said

the mixed
time

        tick

        to      to
        to      tock

              tock

a lonely minute

sightless
i see

                                                she said

the lack of it

& open to all the
specious vagaries

            we
converge
a dusty second

invisible

this hall of several tortures

# alarums don't bring rain she knows

oh my wild
root
                                          she exclaimed

my dry sand
feet and withered
arms all
august & forest flames
                                          she cried

a curse
on the man
& a burning
edge

            go

                    now
with your last
strange day we
will not copy

reuben woolley

# turn a hole what else does she do

                                        she opens holes

                                        in spaces

to this irreverent
dust
     a
conglomeration
of people & people

& people

         & things

circulate
                                        she sees

a fairground / a
battle site / a three-
part list

i'll add a next one

weeeeeee

the merry-go-round
the central eye

you buggers

## this hall of several tortures

feel

a restless earth
a tiresome rock

a universe

collapsing

reuben woolley

# came lightning she saw

walk over
burning
        they do
pull in clouds & blow
a skyfall again

                                                    she knows

a failing
of quickness a
        slight

                hesitation

i can't see you
in this air
                                                she said
i don't feel
a way

        a bridge is no
simple
cry for saviours

        & walls
            flow
into water / into
fire

> this hall of several tortures

# time to go never she cries

walk
        darkly.the moon
is very old

here a pulse &
here a thin knife

        where they promised
heaven / they turned down
the sound

& now I look
for small voices

whispering

    loud

                              she says

i travel
in the whole tumultuous
mess of it

patient

                              she is convinced

of this i am shell
& empty

unmoving.it's a layered
thing &
i'm looking at nothing

this hall of several tortures

# double histories

                i watched him etch
                in thin water
                      our sons
                      our daughters

                                      she bent the air

there are no
glorious
spoils just

        bones
for dry streets

                i step through
                where all the scenes
                          fail
& only death
has a name

        who

comes quiet
a dusty face.who
moves in layers / wrapped
in dark hours

really

                                                             a solution of sounds
                                                             she said

do they think
of permanence

                    i do not want
                    my ghosts

                    in broken times

the black sand
spills
under black
cliffs

                    think me a city
                    think me a distant
                    storm

                    approaching

these are faked shadows

fucking every sign
of life

this hall of several tortures

# ultimate simulations

breathing together

the same
   air / unseeingly

        she complained

no touch
no

  personal

rub-a-dub me.growing
in different

waters

  & gardens are only
for nettles
& dock leaves

    the ship
& all waves flow
in crossed
directions.remember

breathe in breathe

                out

& dead bones waiting

we are
cruel survivor

this hall of several tortures

# descry a world / a world she cries
(a poem for two voices)

                                                                            she says

we
chase them where
impulse
          can't see
through skins

they mirror

just look
at us trying
make a thing called

                        happy

& scratch the little fucker

                        burning

there's no concern
for human comfort
not here                         not here

let winds come            let winds through
blow off                         blowing

the last luxury              down
hotel                             a home or more

# sand count

eyed i am i see
in
      cracked
      glass
                                        she said

a smother of sights
& wondering / lost
in new lines / new lies

they sing me all around.i'm not
a someone's solid sold
or bartered

        here
& bitten
by  tales of rotting splendour

let me rest in the ever night
close my white eyes
a last & tiring hour

this hall of several tortures

# singularities i cannot touch she confesses


lying
in shadows behind
their eyes
                i am
not blind
                              she owned

see them move
a daily round
a thin skin
covering
                & fixed
an earth they don't escape

                              she explored

                              sharp

                              the nothing / between

in sand &
atoms is this
a human display &
power a resistance they reject
such parallel sight

# words i don't hear she said

they tell stories
they do

        tell stories
in their heads.it's where
they live

                                        she said

& listen
to the counting of it all / the surge
their silence

            missing
their

      lost histories scrabbling
i hear

it's not a pleasure

      sleep &
let them out.it's when
i know

come sound you fuckers

just once
    one first last time

this hall of several tortures

# sweet dreams she whispered

they say now
is not time
for soft display.you

                      never
see a swirling world
about you

                              not
                              to any particular
                              she advised

where breath
is a luxury.in

& out
my dears.just

        look
at the gilded eyes

                following

& here we are

        alive

with all its spurious
meaning / hardly

      assembling
missing pieces

the cracked face
of a tired earth

this hall of several tortures

# they walk the way they go she said

a blank

       white

                            she noted

it comes.quick
the oldman said

& what the bells added.i
could dance
to that
      a multiple
step / they pass

      gravely

this is
celebration

& their death goes before

# party decorations

this is where i'm
still breathing
                                                            she said

listen to me
wheeze a slow
        sign
of life

they're hanging
all my body
fluids to dry
        see them
swing & it's a windy day

i'm creaking
a last leathery will.don't
touch

      & slowly
turn to fix
a face

        a lonely stare
for ravens to dine / the manners
of stropping beaks

| this hall of several tortures |

                       my eyes

                                          she said

are curious appetizers / are
the final

liquid
appeasers

## closing doors on present spaces

come to me in words
                                                          she said
naked.here
the skin is thinner
          & light
comes down in pieces.i'm
waiting

        it is my central conceit

i'm slipping in
through dark water
          burning
               & even
the swans are not white the same

                                        it is her real
                                        like stepping through walls
                                        & always
                                        isaiah went this way
                                        scrolling up a distant heaven

higher daddy
push me higher.i'm
a bag of chemistry
flying

## this hall of several tortures

        & here's
a bauble of knuckles & stones.give
me music for an exit

                                there lie her children
                                uncollected

let me rest on my headstone / a
lucid freeze
in this thick wonder

& came the ould feller / the
man of smoke / dressed
in his twirling skirts and reeking
                    i don't want
a tired death / i'll leave
in arms & a cup to hold.it
overflows our cracked design

& he's taking off the shine
                oh where
is a help when all the rooms
are empty

                              this is her pure
                              redundancy

i'm here for the closing

my broken body in the wind

reuben woolley

where they measure in holes

nine
millimetres
& red

www.ingramcontent.com/pod-product-compliance
Lightning Source LLC
Chambersburg PA
CBHW051658040426
42446CB00009B/1200